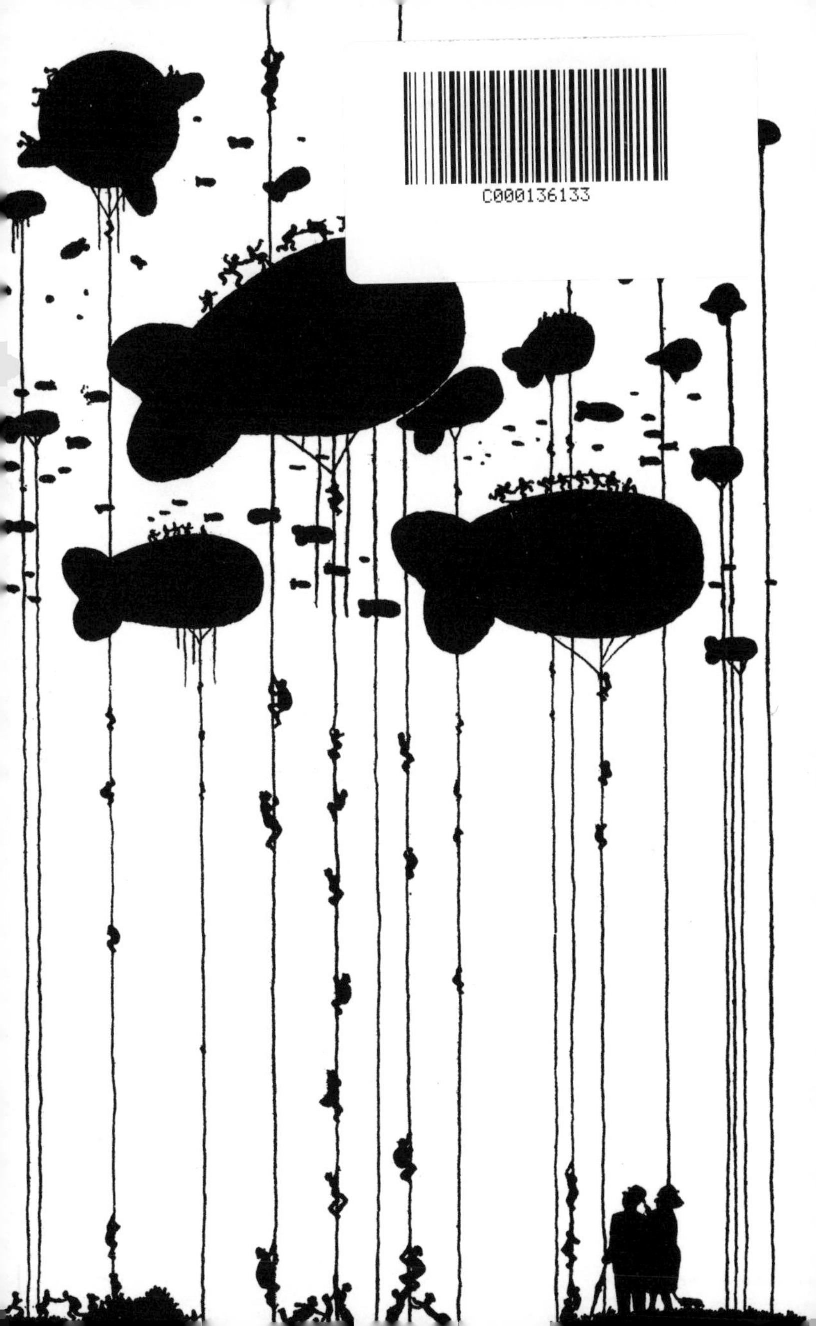

HEATH ROBINSON's

HOME FRONT

Unobtrusive cloth economy

More cheerful and musical air-raid warnings

HEATH ROBINSON's

HOME FRONT

HOW TO MAKE DO AND MEND IN STYLE

By

W. HEATH ROBINSON

and

CECIL HUNT

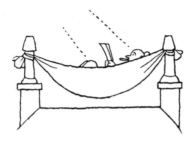

Sunbathing

This edition first published in 2016 by the
Bodleian Library
Broad Street
Oxford OX1 3BG

www.bodleianshop.co.uk

ISBN: 978 1 85124 444 7

First published in 1939 by Hutchinson & Co. Ltd.

Cover design by Dot Little at the Bodleian Library
Designed and typeset by Roderick Teasdale
in 11.5pt on 11.5pt Tw Cen MT Light
Printed and Bound in Great Britain by TJ International Ltd,
Padstow, Cornwall on 90gsm Munken Premium Cream

British Library Catalogue in Publishing Data
A CIP record of this publication is available from the British Library

Anti-splinter spectacles

CONTENTS

*The allotment holder who spent too long
wondering what to do next*

*Well-known painter plumming the
duff when plums are scarce*

Illumination economy

*The magnetic method of dealing with
the shortage of pea-sticks*

INTRODUCTION

If anything were needed to underline the certainty of victory in this war, it is the fact that our humorists were immediately enlisted. In peace we jog along quite comfortably with the unconscious humours of our politicians, but in war every need becomes more imperative, every liver more liverish, every heart more hearty. Even pence become pensive and income is a yearly tax. Never were these things more true than in this present campaign.

Long enough ago to be a dusty answer, a Prime Minister stated that our frontier was on the Rhine. This was a Lorelei that should have been stifled at birth, because every Briton knows that the frontiers today are the cloisters and the hearths of every village and township in the Empire.

The enemy sees these buildings only as targets for insane destruction. He cannot see the inmates, for his eye of faith has always had a cataract, and no one, not even the founders of the tottering edifice of totalitarianism, has suggested that a sense of humour is one of its foundations. They have no leaven in their *ersatz* bread in Germany; it sticks in everyone's gills but their own. Whereas, in this country, if bread were rationed to a crust apiece, there would still be levity about its distribution.

Intelligent collaboration

INTRODUCTION

An ingenious shelter gadget for awakening those who do not hear the "all clear"

It is that levity which enables the mighty Home Front to be disciplined and marshalled so that it becomes a force which nothing in this world can shake. As the old woman said when she contemplated her Anderson shelter: "It'd take more than 'Itler to get me in that!"

Such willingness does more than rule the waves, but even willingness needs guidance, as the centipede said in the shoe shop. And who could be a better instructor in the art of making the best of things than Mr. W. Heath Robinson? In the Great War his humour was so successful that he was not even mentioned in despatches, though it was mentioned gratefully in thousands of letters home. It was taken so seriously by the enemy—the same old enemy whose chief export is war—that courses on British psychology for German officers were based upon Heath Robinson's presentation of the alleged British traits and temperament.

Most of our national institutions are venerable, but Heath Robinson has an eternal elasticity that often

Safety

puts a severe strain upon his braces. He has also a brain that purrs when it is stroked. I count it a privilege to be a humble assistant in that national service. For never was humour more necessary, never was instruction more valuable than in these days when even the worm in your own garden may turn against you.

Making the young war-minded

But there is no worry in worms, no peril in parachutists, no fear in the Fifth Column, no rigour in rationing, no bother in the black-out that cannot be confounded by following the brilliant wit and practical instruction of that archbishop of artifice, Heath Robinson.

When he was appointed Minister for Home Comforts, at the outbreak of hostilities, he nominated me his principal secretary. It is a matter for keen regret to us both, and to a large public, that his collaborator in so many books, K. R. G. Browne, has passed on— the victim of an accident directly attributable to war conditions. But Heath Robinson and I are old conspirators; we respect each other, even in the presence of publishers. There are worse foundations for collaboration, and we are at one in focusing our beams upon the happy issue out of all our difficulties.

As the devil said to Noah, "It's bound to clear up!" Meantime, we offer you this umbrella of humour with some hope, and, we trust, your confidence.

The musical respirator

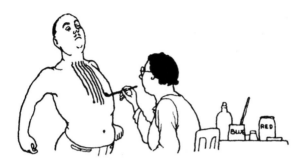

Dealing with an anticipated shortage of striped shirts

A. R. P.

Ever since Napoleon marched on his stomach, and Josephine turned rusty when she was left out at night, war has resolved itself into a question of comfort and stainless steel.

Mr. Heath Robinson was appointed Minister for Home Comforts long before torn up treaties started the European paper-chase. His portfolio is inscribed "Make the Best of Things", with a lion rampant in the top corner and a bottle of milk of magnesia in the bottom pocket.

He was, of course, offered several posts. There were those who suggested that he should be cemented into the Maginot Line as a living symbol of the Allies' unity, and used as a hat-stand by week-end trippers. There was a heavy, almost indigestible backing in the

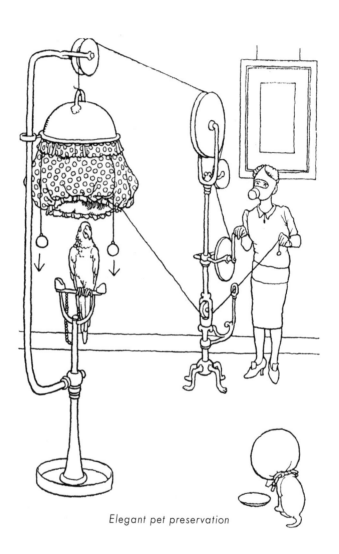

Elegant pet preservation

Cabinet that he should be sent as a neutral observer to Ceylon, but Hitler immediately intimated that he would regard the move as an unfriendly gesture and the motion was dropped. Which was just as well, for Heath Robinson is needed at home. As Minister for Home Comforts he soon made it his business to put every man and maiden at their ease and every lock, stock and barrel at the "Ready". With that quixotic chivalry which makes the Englishman tolerate the Scot, and with the characteristic support of our gallant friends, he turned his attention first to the pets. With the nation's interests firmly at heart, he turned his fine mind to the problem of the tortoise. He gave gentle thought to the slugs, but came to the conclusion that nudists must be left to face bare facts themselves. But tortoises found in him their saviour. After all, a few minutes' warning of a raid is not much for a tortoise, even if it is listening, but with the Ministry's vest-pocket gas mask and Heath Robinson's adapted dish-cover as a shelter, none but the most callous would allow a tortoise to take the wrong turning. Besides, it makes meat rationing exciting to feel that a dish-cover which once gave dignity to scrag end of mutton may now be covering real turtle.

A shelter for the slender

17

Next to Hyde Park Corner, parrots are a prominent national asset, so Mr. Heath Robinson gave them early attention. It is generally accepted that the most moving of Shelley's unpublished poems begins:

> I think that I shall never see,
> A parrot courting in a tree.

Parrots, like aspidistras, landladies and toothpicks, must be preserved if there's always to be an England. And the H.R. dish-douser ensures not only preservation from attack, but nothing is more conducive to egg-laying than this humane war-time appliance. With keen appreciation of the need for economy its inventor has allowed the parrot's own stand to form the main structure. To it is added a simple yet astonishing system of pulleys and pedals which lower the dish-cover over Polly's head. This ensures safety and the flounce of material which depends from it guarantees romantic ruminations or devotion to duty according to whether it is made from Mother's muslin or Father's serge. Experience has proved that dish-covers which normally obliterate a baron of beef or a peer of pork are most appreciated by pedigree parrots who are keen to make the best of it. One, after a trial trip in his extinguisher, shattered his hitherto ecclesiastical record by asking "Why the devil wasn't this blue-pencil war on when I was courting?"

Treatment of the less intractable pets, such as cats, dogs, husbands, etc., will present few difficulties to most readers, but if any are in doubt Mr. Heath Robinson has prepared a special illustrated leaflet on the subject which may be obtained from the Ministry

The vicar's air-raid shelter

for Home Comforts (Raspberry 1212). It is entitled "With Clive to India, or The Incidence of Sand Fly in Piano-Accordions."

With the full life of the nation thus assured, Mr. Heath Robinson turned his thoughts to the well-being of the individual. Now the simplest way to make the best of things is to make war conditions correspond as nearly as possible to peace-time conditions. Imagination is not expected of the ordinary Cabinet Minister, but Heath Robinson is no ordinary being. He has shown how even the Anderson shelter can be made to acquire the personality of its occupant. A decorative steeple can be added which, when topped by a bald rooster, gives immediately a suggestion of the parish church. If a spare stopped clock is added to the vicar's shelter it can provide all that the multitude asks of the church in time of peace.

But even such a shelter and a stopped clock are not always sufficient to guarantee *joie de vivre*. The *sine qua non est* is the perfect gas-mask. And that cannot be acquired without a test.

Testing the gas-mask

The egg

But like all the best things in life, the test is free. How entrancing the test can be is made clear by Mr. Heath Robinson on page 20. A good official test can be obtained by facing a warden, with your mother or your wife waiting with the candle for the backwash. If played before an income tax collector or a landlord it should not be attempted after a heavy meal and the candles should be replaced by an electric light.

Passing from the individual to the community, many home-lovers' societies have co-operated with their local councils in the provision of more imaginative and more musical air-raid warnings. There is much to be said for the normal "Annie's Anguish". Even at rehearsals it has been known to clear bars before closing time, but it is well known that wars are not waged by lounge lizards and the general public prefers something much more sportive. There are those who think that

Warden comfort

Messerschmitts should be heralded by extracts from Mendelssohn and Dorniers welcomed by a few bars from Delibes. But these are perhaps the particular. Most districts are rightly satisfied to make the best of it with Heath Robinson's Symphony Siren which is depicted on page 2. With the brass model a selection of music is included and with all models a plug for the horn to prevent deterioration by rain. It is unfortunately necessary to underline what should be obvious, namely that the plug should be removed before the alarm is blown. In Turvey Tipple the chief warden endeavoured to blow a gavotte without ascertaining that the horn was unplugged. His death was irritating, as he was secretary of the local slate club and never thought of replacing the funds until the first week in December.

But that was merely a misuse of what in other lips can be a delight and a refreshment.

Wardens with no ear for music may care to make more than the best of life by investing in the Heath Robinson Help-for-all-Auxiliary. By reason of its appurtenances it is invariably outside the Motor-Cycle category—and the "Red Lion". It is rated, like the duck-billed platypus, as an amphibian because it goes as well on water as it does on petrol. It is all a question of gradient. An examination of its design will show that it enables a warden not only to be comfortable in all weathers but to pour out succour to all and sundry. The furled umbrella is, of course, not to protect the warden, who is already subsidized. It is unfurled in the case of rain or dew to prevent the split pea from swelling in the whistle and thus causing an obstruction.

The bottle nesting under the south strut is, by connoisseurs, filled with red wine, which thus acquires the essential gentle warmth from the near exhaust-pipe. Those who prefer port may find that in the hands of a too zealous warden the Auxiliary causes a disturbance of sediment. This can be removed by putting the Auxiliary gently into reverse, when the flame of the spirit kettle acts as a discreet headlight. The proper headlight can then be extinguished by foot and its cover removed. The port is then strained through the cover into the fitted tea-cup. Vintage ports have been found particularly responsive to flannel covers as they absorb more lamp oil.

HEATH ROBINSON'S HOME FRONT

Mr. Heath Robinson and I spent many evenings not so much in the perfection of the Auxiliary mechanically (for all his machines are mechanically and spiritually invulnerable), but we were determined that it should meet all the warden's needs, or at least such needs as could be met in the performance of duty. We attended innumerable courses of lectures and from the conflicting advice sifted the essentials. One need was common to all: the warden had difficulty in remembering the answers. One had a crib inside his cigarette-case, another had the key formulae pasted on the face of his watch. So we decided that a book of rules must be provided with every Help-for-all-Auxiliary. It is easily removable and can be jettisoned without losing steam. Its rest can then be used as a pillion for fair passengers, when all rules go by the board and all Auxiliaries by the darkest roads.

Those who find themselves too old for active national service can still enter with zest into the Make the Best of Things Movement. After all, in addition to home fires to be kept burning there may be others we shall want to put out. And in this elderly men with ripe but straight breath can be a national asset. The H.R. Keyhole Fire Extinguishing Fitment is no mere toy. It is exempt from Entertainment Tax because it swells the whisky profits. The Fitment can be hired by municipal authorities, who can recover their expenditure by letting out advertising space on its screens. As in all advertising, discretion is necessary. One Fitment was ruined in Godalming by the advertising of such seductive lingerie that the first pupil drew his breath instead of exhaling and the candle-flame was drawn irrevocably through the first keyhole and was no more seen.

Practice in the extinguishing of a fire in its early stages through the keyhole

Whiling away the time during an air raid

Those who find their breathing disturbed by the tinkling of a bell can fit the alternative indicator supplied with each Fitment. It consists of a raw egg which, when licked by a well-directed candle-flame, poaches itself in the receptacle beneath.

There is no need for anyone's capacities to be ignored in this war; Mr. Heath Robinson is here to make the best of everybody.

That is why he went to some pains to prove by personal experience how enjoyable a *thé dansant* can be in an air-raid shelter. The pains were acquired during a test in a shelter that was under water. Except that a hall-stand is an unjustifiable encumbrance, the congestion is in no way inferior to that found in the most expensive night clubs. If Hesitation Waltzes are introduced, there need be no interval for refreshments. Couples hesitate at the buffet; and sandwiches cut in triangles can be grasped, held jointly and eaten simultaneously.

Dancing in such circumstances acquires a new significance and it is not difficult to understand why the Olympic Games were instituted as a relaxation.

If the atmosphere becomes not only friendly but as clinging as a relative the door can be opened and aviation within a radius of five miles will be impossible.

There are always, of course, those men who cannot or will not dance. It is not our policy to intern the abnormals or to give them political rank; rather do we humour them and thus get the best out of the second best.

For them Mr. Heath Robinson has evolved the rules of Cricket in a Confined Space—eminently suitable for long sojourns in an air-raid shelter. A ball is unnecessary and may even be dangerous, though a rubber sponge will sometimes stimulate the thirst, but sufficient room must be left to allow the batsman to swing his bat and for the umpire to wear a hat. If the teams remove their jackets they are easily recognizable, and Mr. Heath Robinson has available on application signboards marked "Pitch Full" for display outside shelters when play has started.

It is confidently expected, however, that some fine weather will be spent in the open air, and maintenance of cricket proper, in its natural element, is vital to the nation's life. Some concessions to safety can be made without in any way scarring the countryside. Just as a mother sheep will succour an orphan if it is wrapped in the skin of her own dead lamb, so will the raiders frolic and forget their bombs when they see the new form of war-time cricket devised by the Minister for Home Comforts.

By the simple expedient of placing a sheep on the back of each player and giving the umpire a smock and a crook, the game, seen from above, looks like an exquisite idyll or a loot of lambs discussing the meatless day. In such circumstances safety is assured to the players and the cow shot comes into its own.

This plan is not so much a question of camouflage as of giving our established religion the setting it has always deserved. But golf is a different matter. That is an imported belief, with no livings held by the Crown, and it is never identified by the enemy as part of Britain proper. For golf, then, camouflage is imperative.

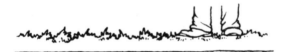

*Healthy exercise during a prolonged stay
in an air-raid shelter*

A cleverly camouflaged game of cricket

"Camouflage" is French for "Mud in your eye!" and some protection is therefore necessary from falling divots. The H.R. Hobby Horse, with club extension aft, is commended to all war-time players. Without it, golf is impossible to many; with it, golf may be probable to some.

Progress is made on the hands and knees, but it is possible to rise at each tee sufficiently to address the ball. Mixed foursomes, with this device, are a simple matter and do not exceed the Government's restrictions on congested areas. It has been found advisable, however, in such foursomes, to mark the fillies with a red feather near the tail, otherwise occasionally two horses are apt to address the same ball and the wrong pairs get lost in the rough.

But the best camouflage, like the warmest charity, begins at home. And, as Mr. Heath Robinson quite reasonably points out, most aeroplanes are above street level, so the roof is the thing. Here, after a study of his suggestions, you will have no difficulty in grasping the principles of disguise. All spare plants, and some that cannot be spared, should be transferred to the roof, together with all boulders that have refused to look like a rockery. Chimneys should be sealed at grate level and filled from above with soil. When the earth reaches the chimney-top it should be levelled off, ploughed lightly, and levelled off again. Trees should then be planted in these natural tree-pots, and if hearths are filled with crinkled paper there is very little danger of roots intruding into bedrooms without appreciable warning. Oaks are not recommended owing to their slow growth, but all species of broom take kindly to soot.

Where time is on your side it is possible to erect a temporary structure above the chimney which can be disguised with foliage, and in the soil itself marrow seeds or bath salts can be sown. The plants will soon be running down the side of the house and, with a little ingenuity, can be encouraged to flower and fruit outside the appropriate windows.

Camouflaged golfer

Camouflaging the house and grounds

If there is any danger of the lawn looking green and tidy from the air, the watering-can should have a tail feather attached to its handle and a ring of potato pushed on its spout. It will then look so like a sitting pheasant that not even a German will shoot it before October 1.

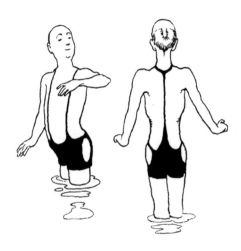

Gents' economy bathing-suits

The ration belt

DOMESTIC SHORTAGES

The Minister for Home Comforts, early in his deliberations, decided that if millions of Eves could be persuaded to play the game of "Making the Best of Things", life would be more exciting—well, anyway, funnier—for all. Because women indisputably possess imagination and a sense of humour—otherwise why bother about men at all? And clearly no housewife who serves up sallow masses and calls them greens can be without vision. That vision must now be enlisted in the nation's service. It should be focused upon home life and the household gods. After all, how much do we really need in life? Or, to put it another way, as a woman always does, how much can we eliminate and not miss?

DOMESTIC SHORTAGES

Take the bedroom first, as every woman seems to start her day there.

Those vallances, for example; they are used only to hide boxes under the bed. And those boxes are up to no good. I turned out one myself the other day and in it discovered two books—*Sir Isaac Newton*, and *The Fair Daughter*—and a baby's bottle. Most unwarrantable promiscuity. The lino or carpet under the bed is probably handsomely new; give it the air—and turn the vallances into underwear. A touch of colour won't hurt. It may help the timid and it will always brighten the Siegfried Line. Lengths of vallance on a base of old tennis net make an admirable dance frock. Think of the joy of serving without hitting the net! Many a tennis player has loved like the deuce for years without ever achieving this luxury.

Then take the pillows, or, rather, don't take them; consider them. Their only purpose is to keep the head comfortably higher than the feet. This can be more simply achieved by halving the lengths of the legs at the foot of the bed.

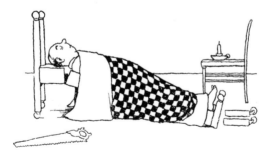

How to dispense with pillows

If they are metal, the sawn-off hollow sections can be used for forcing radishes on the war allotment. Care should be taken to remove the castor and bearing before pressing them into service as even the weakest radish likes room to repeat.

If the bed legs are wooden they can be stored as fuel or put through the mincer and served as a breakfast cereal. By this means more hay is available for the tanks and vital shipping is released for work of national importance.

The pillows themselves can be put away until the peace, thus saving soap. In times of national emergency, pillow-slipping is a preserved occupation. The pillow-cases can be offered as patchings for barrage balloons. There is evidence that, where they have been so employed, married enemy pilots have been seized with nostalgia and gone into reverse immediately. More than one bachelor pilot has stalled his engine.

The feathers need not, of course, be sent to the Balloon Boys. The larger ones (the feathers, not the Boys) should be dredged and kept as garnishings to give atmosphere to Bombay Duck.

Those who find their Real Down Pillows to be in fact stuffed with flock can make omelettes with it or feed it to the goldfish. In both cases the effect is to make stomachs more worthy of war efforts.

But it is in the wardrobes that economy is really exciting. There the game of "Making the Best of Things" becomes a pastime only comparable with refusing to buy a new hat.

The wise wife tackles the man's wardrobe first. There is more room to move. His evening dress is clearly a luxury; particularly "tails". There is, of course, nothing in a man's wearing "tails" except an absurd waste of material and the inference that his contours don't take too kindly to a dinner-jacket. Now "tails" depend for their effect upon two factors. From the front they depend upon the cut of the coat; from the back, upon the tails. But why *tails*? The effect can be established by a single tail, as the Minister has powerfully demonstrated. The second tail can, and should, be removed. A feather stitch will stop fraying and the lining of the removed rudder should be opened at the top. You have then, without any expense, an admirable coffee-cosy or a fitment that can be sent to regimental bandmasters as a cornet-case.

Inconspicuous method of meeting the dearth of braces at Ascot

Care should be taken to remove gloves and cachous from the pocket in the tail. One tail that had not been carefully examined was sent to the bandmaster of the 5th Arguileshire and was eagerly appropriated by the cornet soloist. But a cachou, unknown to the instrumentalist, became lodged in the cornet's aft sump and the soloist was confined to barracks for contempt of court.

But it must be stressed that extra cornet-cases are of no service to our cause if the givers are thereby incapacitated. If wearers of tails are susceptible to rheumatism or spasms at the base, care should be taken to remove the *right* tail, so that an identity card or petrol coupon can be worn in the hip pocket as a protection.

Dress shirts are holding up acres of linen that might be setting the sails of victory. No one in wartime wants his tail between his legs and no man who has danced without a tail will deny that the national service afforded by its gift far outweighs any necessary small adjustments. Once the dancer remembers to make allowance for bias when cornering, his efficiency is not impaired. Indeed, with some partners, the ability to bank steeply is a recommendation.

While this salutary raiding goes on in the man's wardrobe, the male barometer obviously registers "Dry". There are two remedies; *a*, a bath; *b*, a drink. But

Economizing hot water

DOMESTIC SHORTAGES

Beer is still the best

soap and water are precious commodities, and no one likes bathing in a puddle. The Minister has anticipated that difficulty by suggesting the Breakwater Bath Mat depicted on page 38. By its means the high-water mark can be achieved at no expense. Those who find that their bath-mat needs cutting to fit the bath should save the triangular pieces of cork thus removed. They make excellent sandwich-filling or they can be fed to teething babies.

Those who know the Minister will realize that beer problems will never get past him. Everyone knows that beer is best when you can grip a tankard, tip it up and, well . . . who am I to intrude upon the poets' preserve? But beer is scarce, or at least the means to pay cash for it are scarce, so the Minister has devised the Tankard Taster, whereby you get all the atmosphere, all the joy of the first taste, and only consume an egg-cup full. It is a profound thought.

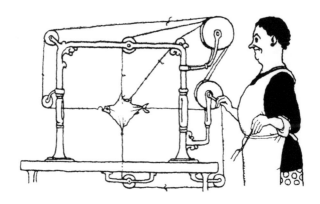

The bloater spreader

Meantime the wife is making whoopee in her own way. She faces her own wardrobe, and no public-spirited Eve can do that without seeing instantly the opportunities for economy. Not one, but two dresses can be hung on

Making the most of the plum ration —

each dress-hanger, thus releasing tons of firewood for Generals' batmen. This economy measure immediately makes more space in the wardrobe. It can be filled with new outfits. This habit has been in force since Eve turned to Adam and said: "My dear, I haven't a rag to put on." It is a highly contagious but not yet certifiable disease.

In the kitchen the wife can work miracles in keeping up peace-time prosperity on war-time rations. The Heath Robinson Plum Pie Pummeller will set the minds of housewives working in the right direction. The Bloater Spreader is a boon. Even a child can use it. Indeed, you will have difficulty in keeping the children away from it. In second gear it will make a bloater look like a dear old sole in twenty seconds.

Now psychologists, and even intelligent people, are agreed that the benefits of food are doubled by our relish of them. And that relish, which releases all the artful little juices, is largely controlled by mental processes. The Minister doesn't claim that the mind has so much domination over matter that you can

— in the plum season

The cycocar, for petrol economy

mistake a sausage for a meat transport, but he does say the principle is sound. It has, indeed, been proved to someone's satisfaction that we do not put mint in a dish of potatoes because we like the mint flavour, but because potatoes have an insipid, unappetizing flavour and the bright green of the mint relieves it.

Yet even green can be overdone, as instance the superb banquet which was made uneatable to hungry guests when experimenters turned a vivid green limelight upon the succulent dishes. It's a question of intelligence. Much can be done with colour, as every woman knows. For years the best hens have been dipping their eggs in coffee before marketing, and what's pert to a pullet shouldn't harass a housewife.

This principle needs impressing. Too many, for instance, bowing to regulations, have bought subdued blue lights, for the simple reason that shops have offered them. As though wars were won by such complacency. Subdued red lights now, while satisfying regulations and economizing in current, suggest at once the Fire Station, and all experts agree that excitement is a marvellous appetizer. A man has been known to eat his own words under a red light and declare himself satisfied.

A focused red beam upon the *plat du jour* can make a Buck out of the mildest Welsh Rabbit and turn rice pudding into the most costly curry.

The Minister is at present engaged upon the production of a set of appetizing lantern slides. With them a background of mixed vegetables can be projected on to the most isolated cutlet and a sizzling

Oil economy

roast chicken can be served by preparing only the bread sauce. Artists who have experimented with the use of these slides have recorded their exquisite pleasure at being able to carve leg after leg off the projected bird without diminishing its attractiveness. As one put it, sagely, "I now understand the feelings of the widow's cruise," which in itself is an advance in a man.

One of the slides expected to be most popular with the masses is that which enables a mock turtle to be projected on to a tureen of egg-water. By gentle movement of the slide across the light it is possible for the mock to swim right through the soup before it is eaten. Thus is achieved an intimacy that even the best soup producers cannot claim.

Care must be taken, however, to see that the slide is removed after the course is finished. One wife removed the lantern to make room for the bread-plate and neglected to remove the slide. As a result a dish of pea soup was projected on to the accommodating neck of the local vocalist. There, for some minutes, it hovered with all the unreliability of an embarrassed débutante, until the maid entered with the fried whiting slide and dropped the lot.

But, as the Minister says, one cannot legislate for unconscious humour. He can but suggest; no wise man ever does more to a woman.

Magnifying the ration

Safe conversation at the hairdresser's

COPING WITH THE BLACK-OUT

If the enemy with his works of darkness thinks a black-out can extinguish Britain's light, he's wrong again. Striking matches have always been a part of the Empire's fabric. In fact, half our strikes are deliberately arranged as an excuse for matches between the police and the workers.

Today, vestas wax strong in everyone's equipment, but striking matches in the street is risky. From the air such lights are apt to suggest glow-worms courting, and this, of course, immediately identifies the county. Only in non-military areas are glow-worms allowed promiscuous mating.

But smokers need not be depressed. The Minister for Home Comforts has designed an admirable pipe-lighting scuttle, depicted on page 48. It can be fitted to lamp-posts, pillar-boxes, or to a stalwart policeman's belt. When erected at a warden's post, a chafing dish is available whereby haddocks can be gently smoked over the top vent.

COPING WITH THE BLACK-OUT

It is even possible to have a luminous keyhole nowadays without anyone casting aspersions upon your nocturnal habits. For those who favour them, there is no better fitment than the H.R. Keyhole-Finder. If by any chance your wife or paid keeper should neglect to light the candle, a lighted match should be carefully pushed through the keyhole on to the ever ready wick. When the candle is burning steadily the keyhole will at once be sighted and the key can then be placed confidently in the hole thus revealed.

From the first day of its operation the black-out has brought into their rightful sphere many garments and materials with a shady past and an even darker future.

How to find the keyhole in the black-out

One old lady, to my knowledge, dashed into the village draper's shop and threw her arms round a black bundle standing by the door.

"Just what I wanted," she gasped. "I thought you might be sold out."

The bundle squirmed.

It was a nun.

"Nun so blind as those who won't see," as you might say, but it shows the spirit. So did the washing-up cloths used by the barmaid of the "Bottled Bodkin" to cover the windows. They showed so much spirit that clients kept pulling them down to wipe their whiskers. It was a touching sight, until the warden called. Then it was touch and go.

A more sensible use of such rich materials is to hang them with other wardrobe warriors in strings across your flooded garden. This admirable ruse, suggested by the Minister for Home Comforts, has the full support of the Ministry for Agriculture and Fisheries, and if used bath water is employed no extra water rate is chargeable.

Parachutist prisoners, to whom Mr. Heath Robinson has outlined the scheme, assure him that

For lighting pipes in the black-out

48

How to await the approach of parachutists
with equanimity

they would prefer cold, or even hot, steel to alighting in the flooded garden of *Chez Nous*, with criss-crossed lines of nappies lapping in the tide.

To be forewarned is, with our enemies, to be forearmed, and several parachutists have been fitted with collapsible submarines as part of their equipment. But it was found that they were apt to cause the soldier's vest to ride up, and in any case it was feared that their underwater speed would not be sufficient to penetrate a neighbour's reserve.

Water gardening, of course, should be supervised by strong swimmers, especially after dark. Wives with paddling husbands are advised to take them with them when they go out in the black-out rather than leave them loose in the house. Such husbands are often inexperienced in the works of darkness, and are prone to be bewildered by traffic crossings. The Cistern-Assister has, therefore, been designed to give all the protection of a tank without its motives. The bought

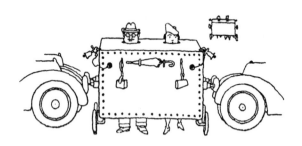

*How to cross the road in safety
during the black-out*

COPING WITH THE BLACK-OUT

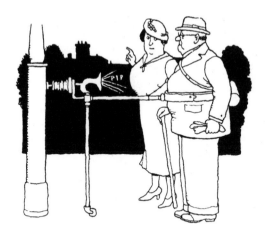

The lamp-post detector

models are fitted with bells to warn approaching traffic, gas-mask hooks and umbrella racks. The best models have no bells as they are so reinforced that traffic which ventures against them recoils to lick its wounds.

Those who prefer to make their own Cistern-Assisters from old water tanks should apply to the Minister for Blue Print No. DF.T42.1940L. No licence is needed and the best pilots are not certified.

Those who are wise will arrange to include in their Cistern-Assister the now well-known Lamp-post Detector. The Cistern-Assisters cannot be taken into small streets or shops and are not welcomed in churches or cinemas. Owners must therefore be equipped for a certain amount of walking and the detection of lamp-posts is essential to comfort.

To avoid embarrassing situations

If you take kindly to lamp-posts but resent indiscriminate human collisions, you should invest in, or manufacture, the Viewless Visor. Shrewdly manipulated it can ensure a skirt in every encounter and make the oldest man feel young.

But when Father hies to post, other fitments are essential.

Going to post has always been a journey of infinite possibilities, but in the black-out these cannot always be controlled. The best way, therefore, is to leave a trail as you go and to follow it upon your return. Care should be taken to familiarize yourself completely with the household oddments scattered. One Tooting resident, mistaking a neighbour's overdraft for his own, picked up the wrong trail and was eventually found addressing a bankers' conference in Aberdeen.

The Minister for Home Comforts, ever anxious to reward good work, has immortalized on page 54 the epic enterprise of Chief Warden Willie Catarrh. Willie was lisping a sonnet at the corner of Pumblechick Place when his swivel eye lighted upon a disturbing beam from the third floor back of Widow Wetweed's guest-house. Spurning the sonnet, he quickly changed his rhythm and exclaimed, "How far that little candle throws his beams!"

Leaving an easily followed trail

With his unswerving devotion to widows' welfare, he did not disturb the offending household, but rose to the occasion. Seated upon a chair suspended in front of the window he applied his natural resources to the emergency and exclaimed with pride: "So shines a good deed in a naughty world."

From time to time, as the warmth became insistent, the warden, following Biblical injunction, turned the other cheek, and when the Fire Brigade arrived he was heard crooning to himself: "I'm to be Queen of the May, Mother; I'm to be Queen of the May."

Thoughtful wardens blocking out a light in order not to disturb the householder's sleep

COPING WITH THE BLACK-OUT

Chief Warden Willie Catarrh has since been appointed Night Very Cross of the Order of the Purple Posterior. His investiture during the black-out was an occasion for much feeling.

For the convenience of chatterbugs

*To prevent light being
seen from above*

The shortage of curates' hats

GENERAL ECONOMY

One of the inescapable privileges of war is the Art of Doing Without—or doing with, without the usual ingredients.

Imbued with the spirit, Mr. Heath Robinson did think of just drawing this chapter to a close, but he decided that the text needed his aid before the reader was exhausted, so he has illustrated it throughout. In any case, it has been proved frequently that not every housewife has the courage to do things without seeing them in print.

It is one thing to be told over the air that you must do without paper, but the shrewd shopper wants to know what she will look like before she trims her sales.

It's the psychology of the thing. Curious creature, Psyche, and if she'd had a bit of paper when she dropped that spot of hot oil on Cupid she might have made mythology more mythterious than ever. But of course it is too late now.

Substitute for paper bags

Not so with the Minister for Home Comforts. He is never late. Before he was shortened he had coined the slogan "Think of the essentials, and then rule them out." And, as you will see, he has applied it perfectly to shopping. Without paper and its rich relative, cardboard, shopping becomes not only more exciting, but infinitely more informative. There is no longer need to speculate upon the smells emerging from next door. You can see the exact constitution of their meal. It is possible that your cutlets came home in the same cauldron as their carbolic. For war-time shopping without paper is nothing if not communal.

The Minister has pictured the uses of the saucepan and the coal scuttle, but they are only tentative suggestions; the field is fertile. If you consider the scuttle too bourgeois, you can always use an *entrée* dish or, for extensive purchases, push the dinner-wagon around the market-place. The only snag with the dinner-wagon, apart from the parking problem, is that it is apt to bank steeply at corners, and overhanging tripe has been known to clog the steering.

For those housewives who already carry quite enough fore and aft, the old two-handled zinc bath has much to commend it for dual delivery. Swung heartily when full of shopping it has been found to command entry into all normal shops and to be respected in the most aggressive queue.

Those who still prefer to walk with their hands free should utilize their pets for paperless shopping. Dogs with a sporting *chassis* are admirable for the transportation of spaghetti, rhubarb and other absurdities of nature, but it should, of course, be laid north and south upon them. Streamlining is essential in war time and to place such commodities east and west is to court traffic congestion and untold catastrophies in the region of lamp-posts.

It is also advisable to arrange the shopping according to the type of dog owned. Spinach gets less matted on smooth-haired types and lentils, that unwittingly leaked upon a sheepdog's back, were found to have gone far too deep into the problem to be suitable for soup where recovered.

It is all a question of common sense and colour schemes; no one with victory at heart would think of weighing down a borzois aristocrat with artichokes or dirty linen, or dream of putting anything but a shirt upon a greyhound. The best shopping dogs are those that can be led, and if the shortage of leather leads is a handicap, the Minister has anticipated that difficulty by the production of "Polarized Polly", a coy belt depicted upon page 60. With this magnetic fitment, care should be taken to wear insulated

Dispensing with wrapping paper

*Scarcity of
leather leads*

underwear, otherwise there is the danger of short circuiting when the dog takes a devious route.

But with or without a "Polarized Polly", you would not trust eggs to any dog. There has never been a real reason, other than prejudice, why this commodity should ever be wrapped. Eggs are essentially decorative and the obvious employment for them is the adornment of man's otherwise drab head-gear. With so many distracting uniforms about, the average man will welcome the opportunity they afford for wholesome self-expression.

One hint is perhaps necessary; it has been found inadvisable to put double yolkers into top hats as they are apt to become broody.

With a careful choice of brilliantine, or the substitution of animal fats, a bacon flavour can be imparted to the eggs while in transit. This will prove particularly welcome when they are poached on meatless days. Those men who normally favour an exotic pomade may find that their eggs lean more to omelettes. Those that lean too much on interrogation should be propped against the Fifth Column and left to speak for themselves.

GENERAL ECONOMY

The use of the hat as an egg carrier naturally absolves the wearer from the usual courtesies of the road, though it is in the interests of economy to obey traffic lights. Personal greetings can be acknowledged by a lift of the left eyebrow or the raising of the right trouser leg to reveal the special Greetings Garter designed by the Minister for this specific purpose.

But while the use of paper must be restricted, there are no limits upon imagination. Indeed, its exercise is welcomed and there would be small chance of winning the war without the continued production of those national indigestibles that have so long been part of the fabric of Empire. Just as there will always be an England, so will there always be Irish stew, bacon and mushrooms, duck and green peas, mulligatawny, crooners and other similar threats to the stomach.

The thing is—will there be adequate ingredients unless we take personal steps to provide them? Mind you, Heath Robinson and I would take more than special steps, we would take plenipotentiaries to see that no crooner was ever hatched again, but digestions differ, and it may be that you cannot contemplate the disappearance of duck and green peas, the missing of bacon and mushrooms. You will see that the Minister feels for you and has designed home-producing units of these dishes. Particularly let me draw your attention to the H.R. Garden Cabinet. If preferred, and the flue is cleaned, a pig can be similarly installed in the

Bringing home the eggs

Duck and green peas

fireplace of the spare bedroom. Care should be taken, however, to remove the family groups from the facing wall as bacon deteriorates if the pig is not temperamentally serene.

The Irish Stew Window Box is simplicity itself, and its ingredients, with the addition of the contents of the carpet sweeper, will also lay the foundations of a fine Minestrone.

But having sated the inner man it is almost impossible to avoid acute appreciation of the button famine. Fortunately it is possible to obtain Girth Girdles which give national security and personal elegance. These should first be fitted, as illustrated, by an expert dietician or by a housewife skilled in the making of beef olives.

If the Girth Girdles are procured in crêpe rubber strenuous exercise can be enjoyed without the necessity for their removal. Indeed, a little trip in the one-husband-power car will soon prove not only who wears the trousers, but how cutely and caressingly the Girth Girdles follow the deflating contours.

These Girdles are made in all shades and have an expansion of three in one. They make the button famine seem a boon and when not in use can be used

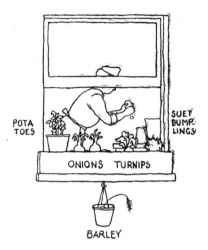

The Irish stew window-box

*A neat garden cabinet for growing bacon
and mushrooms*

as excellent catapults against parachute troops. Alternatively, if suspended in a breezy thoroughfare, they will yield all the airs of Jubal's lyre—and many another liar, too, if care is not taken to remove them before darkness drops in.

But that is straying to a more militant theme, which is the subject of another chapter. . . .

Elegant way of dealing with the threatened button famine

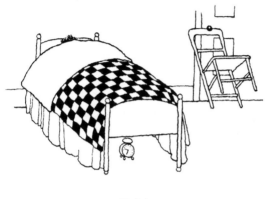

Holiday

HOLIDAYS AND RECREATIONS

There is no doubt that if you have read as far as this without going into a coma or the local, your imagination has been stimulated. And that, as psychologists would say, is significant. Because this question of making the best of holidays requires nothing more than imagination. After all, for years millions have been imagining they have enjoyed their holidays. It is all a question of mental adjustment, and in these days that state must be achieved without expense.

It is a simple process. The first step, in view of the varying interpretations put upon holidays by different people, is to consult a dictionary. The answer is that a holiday is "a day or period of rest from work".

HEATH ROBINSON'S HOME FRONT

Punting in the security of your own back garden

Nothing, mark you, about stumbling over tanned torsoes, nothing about exposing astrakhan chests to sea breezes, nothing about climbing five thousand feet to enjoy a cheese sandwich that has been curdled by the unruly heat in the small of your back. Not a mention about dashing two hundred miles a day in order to pay more for poorer beer. In fact, no mention of the innumerable crazy exertions which custom has caused to be known as holidays—just "rest from work".

That's simple enough, even in war time. Indeed, the Minister for Home Comforts feels that he has only to suggest and the nation will fall in. But perhaps that is not happily expressed. Mr. Heath Robinson has long been accepted as a finer bracer than a Gin Sling or a Maiden's Prayer. I, for one, prefer him to reinforced concrete as a garden ornament.

What I mean is, he wouldn't presume to dictate the form your war-time holidays should take; he wishes merely to suggest; merely to open the gate to fresh woods and pastures new and leave the rest to your stimulated imagination.

"Go to it!" as Mr. Herbert Morrison says; holidays may never be more exciting, certainly never less expensive than the recreations of those who make the best of things.

The joys of motoring without consuming petrol

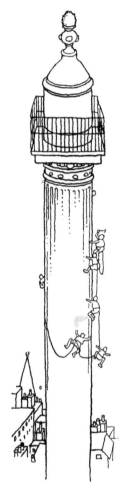

For centuries thoughtful people have refrained from going to the cow for milk. They have let it come to them. Why, then, ravish the petrol supplies and impede the military by touring for a holiday? All that you want to see, and probably more than you would normally detect, can come to you in panorama form and be unwound by a couple of serfs at any speed you require. Such panorama as the Minister has here depicted can be erected by local authorities in public places or they can be hired by the individual citizen and displayed on private ground. They are not liable for entertainment tax but should be taken in at nights in order not to mislead the enemy.

An enormous variety of panorama is available. The railways, shipping companies, and the missionary societies have given freely of their resources and many industrial firms have added scenes of their works'

Monumental mountaineering

processes. It is thus possible from the comfort of your own back seat, to visit Greenland's icy mountains and India's coral strand simultaneously, to dive for pearls or to climb mountains so realistic that the sweat breaks through on the forehead of the holiday maker.

Such panorama may be appropriately followed by an educational scene showing the brewing of beer and concluding with close-ups of the bar of the "Curtained Kidney". Those who wish to linger in such delectable surroundings have only to ask the winding serfs to pause, or, if necessary, to go into reverse. Then the beer will return politely to the tankard, the tankard to the barmaid, the barmaid to the barrel, the barrel to the brewery. It is a beautiful and economical thought which, but for the war and our determination to make the best of things, might never have been released to this thirsty world.

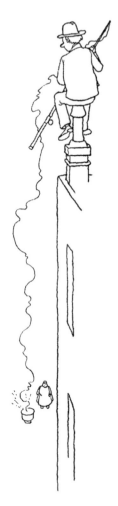

Casting for goldfish

An inexpensive —

Those who are not happy apart, even on holiday, can plan an inexpensive family holiday on the cavalcade lines here depicted. The unit is entirely self-contained and if gearings are carefully adjusted no one need work except father. Care should, however, be taken to traverse only wide roads as some difficulty may be experienced in cornering. One such admirable outfit found that on a steep gradient its leader entered a military area before the catering department in the rear had got out the drinks. The result was that father and mother were interned and the young people, further aft, were uncoupled and surrounded by Parashots.

As the maid said, when the sergeant had inspected her surroundings, "Life will never be quite the same again!" And what finer tribute could anyone conceive to an inexpensive holiday?

But then, this war has undoubtedly produced a sense of unity, community and impunity. What I mean is, we are all in the same debt, even at holiday time, so it is up to our local authority, whether it be city or hamlet, to cater for our distraction as well as for our detention. There is every civic reason why the old standards of

HOLIDAYS AND RECREATIONS

— holiday

living should be maintained, so long as they are shared by more people. This is known as MacPhootum's Law of Equality. It is unaffected by wars, holidays, or reasoning. But it is every justification for thinking that those, for instance, who have been used to big game shooting in the past should still have more opportunities and less motive than the Parashots provide.

Besides, in towns particularly, there is likely to be so much competition for the winging of parachutists that self-expression will have little scope.

Several municipalities have therefore authorized roof shooting. Care should be taken to choose well-mannered or pensioned chimneys, as a sudden rude gust of smoke has been known to deter even accomplished shots. Experience has proved that it is also prudent for the beater or catapulter to wear a cap of conspicuous hue. Alternatively, the cold bird should be given vivid tail feathers. These latter not only ensure a happy landing but eliminate all risk of confusion.

In less exalted circles those who like not only to go to the dogs, but are prepared to pay for such disruption, can erect an admirable track on the compact lines

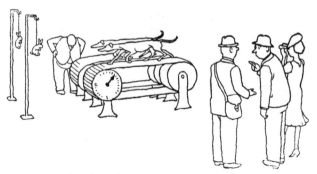

Greyhound racing in your own garden

depicted on this page. Provided that garage hands are not allowed to interfere, the mechanically minded in any village can erect such tracks quite simply from stock in hand.

When the dogs are off duty the tracks can be used as friction massage machines for matrons. Some have

Roof shooting

found the antics of the matrons more exciting to watch than the dog races, but that is entirely a question for the individual.

In inclement weather the Museum Mooch offers a delectable holiday. Do not be dissuaded by past associations. The war has given impetus to a movement to humanize museums and to add the personal touch to much impersonal history. Even the cold comfort of statuary can be made to pulse with life. After all, Venus had hot blood in her veins, and, I dare swear, a nifty new spring outfit occasionally. It is only the blindness of pre-war curators that has caused her always to be represented as a stolid matron with the expression of a woman reading a time-table.

But now statuary is no longer dumb. Why should it be? Cromwell, besides the wart on his nose, must have had crinkles in his conscience that would have made purple patches in even Milton's prose.

The holiday of today can present to you in fascinating form not only the hall-markers of history but the local worthies who have hitherto been little more to you than a drinking fountain or a memorial hall.

Coventry has long been cashing in on Lady Godiva's schoolgirl complexion, and other centres are now sensibly allowing their celebrities to take the air.

Making the British Museum more interesting

Crowds that Blackpool might envy have flocked to see the original Lancashire Hot-Pot which has been dredged from the Manchester Ship Canal and the exhibition of the first Cornish Pasty in Helston has put the Floral Dance into perfumed retirement.

Local industries, such as reglazing the station bun, and giving a roland to Bath Olivers are now depicted in moving scena in the appropriate museums, and separate tables, elastic tariffs and long walks to the sea can still be indulged in by the conservative.

In fact the nation has risen wonderfully to the effort of entertaining those holiday makers who are determined to make the best of things. Everywhere,

The joys of bathing at home

the Minister is convinced, holiday makers will now return to their work with eagerness. And no one could ask more than that of the most expensive holiday!

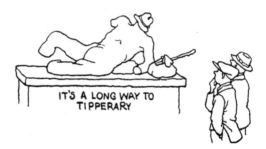

Mechanical rumour-checker

INDOOR RECREATIONS

There are times when Heath Robinson ceases to be Minister for Home Comforts and I cease to be his Principal Secretary. Then we salute the sentries, leave more or less of our personalities on the barbed wire and are escorted home by tanks.

There is much to be said for tanks as escorts. They are singularly impersonal and they look straight ahead, but they are not conducive of ideas! At least, not the ideas that the nation expects of us as a Ministry. These are most frequently hatched in Heath Robinson's studio which, after a time, becomes quite intelligible. The studio, I mean, not the hatching. That is an intimate process which even the Premier has not asked to overlook.

The studio is a snug affair, cryptic with mirrors so that you can see yourself coming before you go, and full of desks, easels, tobacco smoke, publishers' follies and other *objets d'art*.

Here, after consulting the stars, the overdraft and the cellar we produce most of our national service. Sometimes he needs a bracer, but generally the Minister flows quietly like the Don until I find myself knee-deep in wisdom and struggling for breath.

But on the question of Social Occasions and Home Amusements we advanced together. We were as unanimous as a Nazi news item.

Battles cannot now be won on the playing fields of Eton, which may be harrowed at any time. This is the war of the cricket on the hearth, but for the winter months alternatives are required. Quickly we alighted upon the Gas Mask Who's Who.

The game of Gas Mask Who's Who

INDOOR RECREATIONS

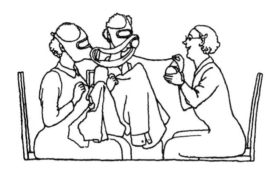

A new use for respirators

As every bachelor knows, the joy of all such sportive games is the forfeits that can be exacted— and the delicious opportunities afforded of putting the persistent in their places. The Minister always remembers with glee the party when Lady Adenoid Autopsia sat lusciously on his knee in the Cushion Game and maliciously he asked his neighbour if he would mind carrying the laundry for a change.

But Gas Mask Who's Who, if it has few opportunities for irony, has more positive attractions. The winner can claim the first hose at Stirrup Snooker, which has health-giving properties unrealized by all who have not swum in it. So popular has the game become that The Stirrup Snooker Association proposes to legislate on the water used in Championship Matches in the same way as the weight of the balls at Wimbledon is prescribed. This might seem to the uninitiated to be a formality, but it was given point when the champion of

Stirrup Snooker

Sluice-by-the-Ouse played in town for war charities. He insisted upon bringing his own water supply and, stringing up for first jet, he so littered the course with sediment that a dredge had to be employed before his opponent could shift his ball out of baulk.

But played thoughtfully and with the best of spirits—lodged for safety on the mantelpiece—it is a game well worthy of our maritime traditions.

Many who have hitherto shown little leaning towards ordinary snooker will be surprised how satisfying a kiss cannon can be at low water. The only equipment additional to ordinary snooker is a waterproof jacket and a certain co-ordination of mind and muscle. One man, so excited when he potted the red, withdrew his hose in ecstasy but neglected to stop pumping with his other hand. The result was that the lighting was extinguished for some hours and the marker demanded artificial respiration in liquid form.

But all games must be approached intelligently. Even the Minister cannot legislate for youthful abandon. Besides, he is romantically minded himself.

Adjoining the Stirrup Snooker beach it is advisable to fit a breakwater and the nearest fireplace beyond can be tastefully decorated, the Minister suggests, to give a sweet nostalgia. A centre-piece

Preserving the "local" colour when you can't go out

of beer-engine handles can be flanked by tobacco plants or empty glasses. Some find clean glasses more inspiring and forward-looking; others, imbued with the "Go to it!" spirit prefer those readily sent by the brewers with three linger-lines etched on the sides.

Those who fear that the taxed tide of beer may affect their fitness should try the new game of Dodging the Stirrup Pump. The Minister's explanatory diagram on page 87 leaves nothing to the imagination except the skill. Students of psychology will be able to detect the rhythm of the pumper's strokes and escape dry and delighted.

When the game was tried out by the Cabinet the only man who soused them all was the Minister of the Interior, who went on pumping without knowing that the nozzle had fallen down. He drove all the ladies into a corner and the Water Board into liquidation.

But there are those who prefer the more gentle recreations. None escapes the Minister's solicitude.

Water to hand at a moment's notice in case of emergencies

INDOOR RECREATIONS

The barrage-balloon settee

Ballad singing, for instance, once despised, is now again in fashion. The Minister suggests that if this trait cannot be suppressed an effort should be made to give it local colour. This scheme has the further advantage that it is no longer necessary to attempt to catch the words. There is also room for humour in such a pastime. Even Miss Luce Larynx is tolerable when singing "Drink to me only with thine eyes", if the piano is decked with whisky and siphons.

Much ingenuity and noble war service can also be incorporated in this atmospheric ballad singing. Anathema Wen, for instance, could think of no local colour for the one song she swore she knew— "Shipmates o' Mine".

The only Ship we knew was closed, and anyway, we valued it too highly to let her sing there. We had no mates we would have trusted with Miss Wen, so for the moment we were stumped. Then a thought was suddenly released in the Minister's mind. He released his cat, Senna, at the same time as she seemed equally moved.

He set Miss Wen upon the aquarium and instantly realized that if every piano-stool were also an aquarium, here was an admirable and artistic way of providing water for emergencies. The idea fulfilled war's demands of preparedness and seemed to have peace possibilities as well.

Several upholstered models were manufactured for the Minister and tried out among his friends. All were well received and atmospheric ballad singing was popularized thereby. The fish thrived and the singing often acquired an added resonance. Jack Hylton's pianist reported that his goldfish handed up a request note for "Rocked in the Cradle of the Deep", but that proved to be an Italian goldfish not used to rough seas.

A suitable fitment for listening to atmospheric ballad-singing is the war-time settee—artistic, economical and patriotic. It is earnestly depicted, complete with barrage-balloon upholstery, on

A new addition to respirators designed for the convenience of bridge players

page 83. The only repeatable *contretemps* we had with ours was when the Mayor, comfortably settled and everything within reach, inexplicably turned yellow. Immediately, the balloon began to rise; or rather that part of it which was not weighed down by civic authority. It was a touching scene of conflicting loyalties which, unfortunately, did not deter the vocalist.

Conservation of timber

Still, it gave heart to the Minister and myself, although it was diamonds which gave us our next brain-wave. We had twenty-eight below the line, seven hundred above and a spare ace under the table. We suddenly saw how vital it was that bridge should not be interrupted by air raids. So when we had collected our winnings we excused ourselves in the national interests and departed to the studio. It was a close call, but after pouring out supper we saw the light. So, unfortunately, did a warden, but he was a bridge player and soon joined our strength.

We quickly designed, and the Home Secretary as quickly executed, a brilliant respirator addition for which no reprieve has been asked, before or since.

If it makes some people's bidding more obscure than ever, the general effect is delightful. The only time it does not contribute to the gaiety of nations is if the wearer has hiccoughs. Experience has proved that this is too often interpreted as "Six Spades" to be remunerative.

*The evening walk need not be discontinued
on account of the black-out*

Such respirator additions can be taken off the gas mask before it is returned to its case, or the mask, with its bridge fitment, can be attached to radio sets for filtering enemy broadcasts.

But even bridge should not be allowed to curtail exercise. To reduce the constitutional or curtail the courting period just because of the inconveniences of the black-out is to play right into the enemy's hands. Forty times round the billiard table is equivalent to the normal stroll, and if Stirrup Snooker is in progress you can close your eyes and feel the spray on your face. The sight of an odd litter-box or two attached to the backs of chairs will encourage you to throw your rubbish on the Prom. with your accustomed holiday abandon.

But even more important, in the Minister's eyes, are the young people. And their walks, of course, depend much more upon company and the moon. Neither need be rationed nor restricted. If it is a trifle more difficult to do a "Hey, nonny no!" in the kitchen, love never has depended entirely upon that.

Lovers, they say, have eyes only for each other, so just a hint is sufficient to give atmosphere to their stroll. A conservatory is a luxury, but a decorously draped table and a plant have been known to produce shining results. With, of course, a synthetic moon. And the Minister, with his usual feeling for the heart of things,

The new game of *Dodging the Stirrup-pump*

Anti-waste measures for the social minded

has shown how that can be achieved, cheaply and without detection.

Those who are prone to giddiness may care to substitute an oblong table, but the walking is, after all, largely a mental process. The moon and proximity have proved sufficient in all cases officially observed. Indeed, several couples after such a wartime stroll have returned to the drawing-room breathless and declared that they would have been home in time if they hadn't had to wait for a bus.

The war-time stroll can be made more realistic if the thoughtful parent or guardian will exercise his or her loving ingenuity. The Minister himself has set a fine example. He is always a master of pulleys, and certainly the master of any axis yet forged, for they are all devoid of humour. He went so far as to convert a suspended clothes-rack into an imitation front gate. That is the spirit with which this war will be won.

It was soon noised abroad that his kitchen had a kissing gate that could be let down at will, a moon that never waned, and sandwiches in the middle of the table. Further, report had it that the lock on the door was reliable.

All sorts of couples called in daylight and dallied until the moon was switched on. Even the gas man called, though it is an electric moon, and brought with him a delectable young woman who, he said, was learning the ropes.

The Minister nodded wisely and put a higher-powered bulb on the moon. Unfortunately, the girl brought a dog with her, which made walking difficult, but during the course of a three-hour stroll the meter was read—very leniently—and romance departed.

By that time there was a queue extending far down the drive. As the Minister and myself live in the same Borough, no other street entertainers are allowed, so Mr. Heath Robinson, with his usual tenderness, took the opportunity to address the walkers on a patriotic theme. Experience proved, however, that in the national interests another scheme should be adopted.

Making the shaving-stick last to the bitter end

The Minister has therefore incorporated a national savings group with his war-walk facilities. While those who run may still read, those who dally must buy a War Savings certificate. In bad weather many are heard to declare that it is cheap at the price.

A way of preserving chocolate wrappings

The man who forgot to cut off the marrow before taking it home

GROWING YOUR OWN FOOD

History doesn't record whether King Richard had an allotment, but then history, as the schoolboy said, largely consists of the shifting of evidence. But there is no doubt that when Shakespeare made him say "This blessed plot!" he said a mouthful.

Since the War these words have been frequently used with such emphasis and eloquence that peas have palpitated in their pods. But as the King went on to say "This blessed plot" really is "this England", and about that there are no two views.

The one view held by all of us is that nothing of her shall be wasted, and hence those with imagination have plotted accordingly.

It really began when the Minister for Home Comforts found himself on the Whitehall Washing Rota. Festooned with wet red tape, he stood looking for something on which to hang it. The main clothes lines from Number 10 to the Treasury were heavy with the underwear of the overworked. So the Minister rolled an eye and observed some bean sticks which appeared superfluous. The beans were rigid with self-importance. They needed no support, for scarlet runners are not often reared in Downing Street, and these were not even scholarship boys.

Simpler than Euclid, thought the Minister; if a bean stick can be used as a clothes' prop, surely a clothes' prop can serve as a bean stick? So simple are the profundities.

The Minister consulted his household experts and while they agreed in principle they diverted his attention to the much more productive field of suburban imagination. The Minister knew the problems of the cities and suburbs. Where was their space to "Dig for Victory?" Where were the plots to produce the green

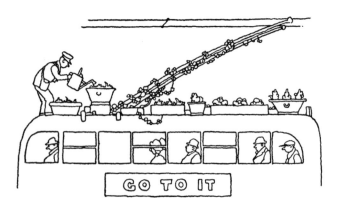

More neglected opportunities in urban districts

The urban lettuce

stuffs? How could saladings be sown in the Strand, or peas be persuaded to propagate in Piccadilly? Parsnips had been tried on Blackfriars Bridge, but had wilted in the rush hours. Mustard and cress had been sown on Stepney shop blinds and radishes planted in Radcliff Highway, but these were untutored efforts and therefore doomed. But then the Minister took charge and at my suggestion issued a pamphlet, from which these ideas are extracted.

At his suggestion and with the co-operation of Kew, several buses were fitted experimentally with concrete urns executed in the Ironic style. Beans, and later vines, were planted therein and encouraged to

Mustard and cress can be grown anywhere

race up the poles and to take their power from the source. Some plants were diffident, others were overcome by giddiness on those routes where there was excessive cornering. But the women conductors soon put them right; a conductoress's caress is just as potent whether she has a bean or a man up the pole.

One wag suggested that with an occasional short circuit it might be possible to produce baked beans in the pod, but taken as a whole, trolley bus horticulture has succeeded. So have the cos lettuce in the gutters of many an enterprising urban district; one of the Minister's greenest thoughts. There was a movement for marrows up the Monument, but the proximity of Billingsgate proved too robust for these temperamental climbers. Yet even this fragrant thought lingered to suggest other things. Many a Billingsgate porter now sacrifices his hat at week-ends for the growing of seakale.

When a large number of our resorts put their piers in patriotic pawn it was found that these structures also took kindly to seakale seeds in those crooks and crannies where winkles used to wander and courting couples were cut off by the tide.

GROWING YOUR OWN FOOD

One man, watching the first harvest of such cultivation, pondered long over the pier seats with their crop of carved initials. He obtained permission to fill these heartaches with soil and produced a loving crop of mustard and cress. He also extracted many a donation from those who came to see their romance thus grown green again.

But of course it was left to Blackpool to go one better. The Minister's Special Emissary surveyed the Great Wheel, looked again, and then convinced himself that it was real. The war has worked wonders with the eye of faith.

Immediately he saw each carriage as a course, and not so much a course as a conducted tour. He perceived that if he planted *hors d'oeuvres* in the first car, bred mixed soups in the second, turned the third into a fish tank and let chickens run riot on the fourth, the Wheel would acquire a new significance.

It did.

True, there was a time when the chickens forgot

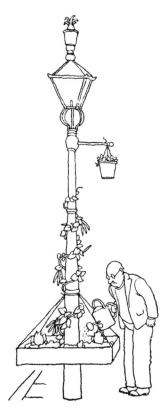

The lamp-post allotment

95

*A gang of carrot thieves at work in
suburban allotments*

that the Wheel had been stopped when they were at
the top. They stepped out into oblivion, but Blackpool
has for many years been turning oblivion into money.
There was another week when the pea soup bred
too eagerly and, abetted by a high wind in Jamaica,
flooded the *hors d'oeuvres*. But those were incidentals
in a considerable triumph.

The speed with which a ten-course meal can be served is a spectacle in itself and the crowds have trebled since it was discovered that, with a wind off the sea, a sustaining repast can be obtained from the spray.

Lower down the coast a councillor, with equal sincerity but less acumen, conceived the idea of using fire-station ladders for growing roller-bandages and hose-pipes. Like many another gardener, he found that they did not come up quite like the picture on the packet. However, the motive was good, and when he embraced a lamp-post with more than usual abandon, this same councillor saw among the stars one genuinely bright light. He saw that every lamp-post was a garden going begging.

It was only a matter of minutes before he had taken counsel's opinion and something for the bruise. At

A simple new machine for thinning out the turnips

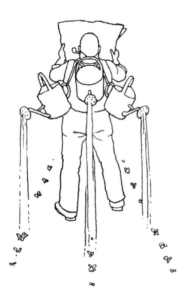

Reading the paper while watering the parsnips

once his urban district acted and the more artistically minded wards planted serried squares of beetroots, carrots and spring onions.

One authority went further. It accepted the suggestion that hot-house plants should be planted in the slits of the manhole covers. It might have been an admirable scheme, but someone mixed hollyhocks with the pumpkin seeds. The results were so belligerent that the hollyhocks bore fruit and the pumpkins bore malice.

And if it is frankly unproductive for pumpkins to be made haughty by hollyhocks, it is sound sense to inflate your marrows with a stirrup pump. Think of the practice—and anyway, who contemplates a normal marrow in terms of anything but remorse?

The Minister has planned and demonstrated many other methods of making allotment work more easy and more productive. Perhaps the one that will come closest to the heart of the digger is depicted on this page; an artful disposition of the prosaic water can.

It not only makes reading possible and probable, but lends itself to much individuality. Only the most artless cultivators water with plain water in war-time. Some have found that the addition of "a wee drap" helps to keep the cabbages in good heart. Others, whose allotments are near military objectives, add a pinch of salt to close the eyes of the potatoes. After all, Fifth Columnists invariably work underground.

But it is the third act upon which a play depends. The First Act is to find unexpected plots, the Second is to exploit them, but all is vanity if the products are not properly exploited on the Kitchen Front.

Shady method of acquiring gardening lore

Carrot soup

Marrow duck

There, fortunately, the Minister has the co-operation of Eve. There could be no more resourceful conspirator. Her marvels of improvisation have astounded every man since Adam. Some have to be seen to be believed. To taste them is to put war in a new light. In the art of making the best of things—as in every other guile— Eve can teach Adam much more than he would willingly learn.

Pumping up the marrow

GROWING YOUR OWN FOOD

Mistaken view as to the uses of an allotment

Examine, for example, the Mock or Marrow Duck. Who but a woman under the Minister's spell could have had such a dream? Its second name is "The Carver's Joy"; no joints to turn the knife edge, no parson's nose to cause dispute, and a breast that can be carved indefinitely.

Indeed, by a little prearrangement with the cook a second socket can be provided in the marrow. Then, after the first six have been served from the breast, the duck's head can be unshipped and re-erected in the stern. This provides an untouched breast from which at least six more portions can be served with impunity.

The parsnip sandwich

In a Regional Competition for snappy substitutes the Minister awarded the Double Yolk to the creator of the Stuffed Turnip recipe depicted below. It is indeed more than a recipe, it is a basic principle. Bound with garden raffia the turnip takes on a new glamour, and when cold it can be used effectively as a door stop. No more than that should be asked of a turnip in any war.

Stuffed turnip

The decoy

MAKING PROTECTION A PLEASURE

The Minister for Home Comforts naturally has an enormous post-bag. There are occasions when it resembles a barrage balloon, and many days on which its contents are lamentably similar.

But now and then something worth reading is not only received, but read. Unlike some Ministers who sleep in Whitehall and have their night's rest at home, Mr. Heath Robinson is . . . but perhaps, without infringing the Official Secrets Act or the Regulations for the Prevention of Saw-fly in Sidlesham, I may tell you more about the Minister at work. There is always a legitimate public for a low-down on a high-up. And in these days of democracy it is right that you should know how Ministerial salaries are earned, or at least spent.

The Minister's house is, of course, a model not only of propriety, but of protection. Even friends have their finger-prints taken by a decorative Home Guard, and tax demands and other foreign bodies are shot on sight.

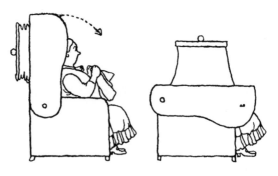

Comfort with safety.   *The new raid chair*

The study, in which correspondence is dealt with, and your complaint lost, is a model of ingenuity. It is on the first floor. The Minister, of course, straps on his parachute every time he leaves the ground, just as he dons his lifebelt when he baths and his diving-suit when he draws inspiration in the cellar or faces his overdraft at high tide.

The most innocent-looking but ingenious fitment in the study is a stirrup pump which has agreed to a divorce in the nation's interests. The nozzle is artfully embodied in the electrolier, while the stirrup and pail are hidden under the desk. By dignified and almost undetectable foot movements the Minister is thus able to extinguish incendiary bombs, inflammable visitors or advancing parachutists without looking up from his work.

The desk itself is, of course, camouflaged. Seen from the front it suggests the Dunmow Flitch before the fighting starts, and from the rear it resembles the Cloisters of Canterbury Cathedral.

As the sign-posts have also been removed from the calendar it is calculated that this room alone will so puzzle the outriders that the invasion will be held up for several valuable minutes.

Two other fitments in the study are worthy of detailed comment because they might be reproduced in many offices with impetus to the war effort.

One is the Salvage Sofa. Disguised as an innocent and indeed luxurious piece of furniture, this sofa swiftly and inevitably analyses and assesses the possibilities of every visitor. The recording dial is, of course, screened on the top of the desk itself. On the dial are recorded the now familiar headings of war: "Waste", "Pigs", "Scrap Metal", "War Bonds", "Lebensraum", "Highly Inflammable", "Minister's Joy", etc.

The other highly instructive piece of furniture is the Letter Detector. Shaped like a tall-boy or maiden aunt, it has a large mouth and innumerable drawers. There the similarity ends because its digestion is completely reliable.

First it selects all those letters whose stamps have escaped the postmark. These stamps it removes in the interests of the Minister's personal economy. Then it sorts the letters into degrees of intelligence and urgency — "Sensible", "Senseless", "Certifiable", and "O.H.M.S."

Only the letters in the first drawer are seen by the Minister. Some of the others have not been seen yet.

The blitzkrieg braces to prevent the trousers being blown off by blast

The Minister at work

The Minister wears his Mafeking trousers and his gas mask while dealing with correspondence. He feels that to secure a balanced view the past should be thus aptly linked with the future. It is a profound thought; so profound that if the ancients had uttered it they would have been rewarded with immortality or at least a half bottle of ambrosia. As it is, the Minister let it slip almost unnoticed with his other pearls.

Now that you can picture the surroundings—and a heartening picture it is in these days—you can imagine the joy with which he read the letter from Sonia Sensible, whose address, embossed with devastating emphasis, appeared to be "Tuffan Tenda", Fallow, Bucks.

The relief of Mafeking was immediate and the gas mask talc dimmed with a cloudy excitement.

The Minister waved the letter at me. I was unprepared for such signs of activity before lunch and I sat down unwittingly on the Salvage Sofa. I landed with such violence that the hand whizzed right round the dial and rang the bell. The Minister, who always treats his staff as he would human beings, insisted that I took an extra tea ration instead of the usual prize of a goldfish in a bowl. "Because," he said, "I want you to keep your hands free. We are invited out."

106

MAKING PROTECTION A PLEASURE

And, indubitably, Sonia Sensible's invitation had no catch in it. It had no reply paid envelope, either, which was a pity, but its news was stimulating.

It said:

We are having an air raid on Friday of next week. We should be delighted if you and your Principal Secretary would join us. Any dress suitable. Music, dancing, light refreshments.

When there are no more shaving sticks

The Minister passed me the note.

The new raid pyjamas

"Sounds just the stuff to give the troops," I said. "We must look up Sonia's past and present. They might have some bearing on the future."

I handed back the note. The Minister surveyed it thoughtfully. At least, I read it as thoughtfully. It is not easy to read the expression of a gas mask, but I know my man.

"There is a post script," he said suddenly, turning the note over.

"We hope," he read, "you will stay the night. We are never quite sure what time the party will start or how long it will go on, so you can stay the night before, the night during, or the night after; just whichever suits you and your sleep best."

The Minister nodded sagely. "She is a woman in a thousand," he said, "a national asset. Accept immediately."

I did so, taking care to dispatch the letter before I turned up the Engagement Diary. Several important events were scheduled for Friday week: a full moon, a quotation by Ella Wheeler Wilcox, three committee meetings, a licence renewal and a blot.

I drew my pen through them all. The second secretary could deputize or apologize, whichever he thought would be most acceptable. The nation's business must come first. We might learn a great deal about the art of making the best of things from Sonia.

We did.

We decided to go on the Friday afternoon.

More cheerful designs for window taping

The cheery game of bobbing the parsnip after a hard day digging for victory

Time would be necessary for observation and we put the nation's needs before personal enjoyment.

And the first thing we observed as we approached "Tuffan Tenda" were the decorative window designs. For months the Minister had been preaching that there was no need to plaster windows as though they were boils on a neck. This adhesive tape, besides being very feeding, offers unlimited scope for self-expression and artistic endeavour. This we adhere to, or we did at the time.

And now here was Sonia putting into practice all the splendid theory we had never tried out. The taping of her windows was exciting in itself. There were excellent presentations of, we presumed, members of the family. We discovered later that the windows of each room depicted their chief occupants. There were slight difficulties, of course. The rigid lines of the adhesive tape made delicate profiles difficult, but such drawbacks were swiftly overcome by artful colouring

Signature tunes enabling friends to recognize one another

effects. There were some rooms, too, that presented difficulties when the scheme was well advanced. The Minister is glad to record them in order that he can set in its true perspective the patriotic spirit that overcame them.

The bathroom, for instance; who should be depicted on its frosted glass?

Father suggested "Venus rising from the waves", but there seemed to be some dispute as to the Venus of the family, and Sonia was not too sure that Venus would be recognized in entirely straight lines. So they compromised by using the family motto, "Sic Transit!" supported by a loofah rampant.

John suggested that it sounded like the first day at sea, but Sonia retorted that that was no bad time to have a bath. To which there seemed no substantial reply.

This was indeed the spirit that made the best of things. Even Cook had been won round. She had been generously depicted on the kitchen window and had been delighted. Then she found that when the window was wide open she appeared to passers-by to be perched on the marrow heap. But, as the Minister was able to persuade her, there are worse sites on which to be broody.

Cook was soon laughing heartily, and indeed the whole house was alive with laughter. Here, indeed, people were making the best of it, and not by blind forgetfulness, for all were engaged in some voluntary service and often in involuntary laughter.

It was not possible to appreciate all of Sonia's charms until after the gas-mask parade, but it was a happy thought to have the masks topped by gramophones playing signature tunes which made introductions easy.

Here was an admirable use for them. It is, of course, advisable when thus utilizing them, to erase the previous inscription completely. One thoughtless guest insisted that it would be adequate if she "just used the other side". She forgot that in the heat of commingling the best flag sometimes furls. We never discovered her real name but her flag flaunted before us all "Cucumber and Cream Cheese", so between ourselves we christened her "Hiccoughs". She was none the wiser; it was that sort of party.

Even the tea tasting they had turned into a parlour pastime. A section of the local Knittery had gathered to welcome the Minister and to take his measurements for bed socks. They swiftly demonstrated the hostess's artful contrivance whereby the communal tea-cup is

Making a cup of tea go a long way

swung round to all with the lavishness of a loving cup in Lilliput. Sonia decked the contrivance with flowers or saladings, according to the season. It revealed a thoughtfulness which I hoped had also been given to the men.

The Minister and I were not disappointed. After the excitement of watching the tea tease we staved off a decline by use of the "Say when", a machine for measuring war-time nips. Mr. Heath Robinson, with that human touch which endears all Cabinet Ministers to the masses, decided that a demonstration would be unnecessary. He would test the apparatus by direct experiment.

We were informed that dinner would be served in the party shelter because some over-riding guests were known to gate-crash at unexpected hours and Sonia did not like her guests to have long hours and short commons.

MAKING PROTECTION A PLEASURE

So first of all we gathered round to see who would be allotted the evening's cigarette. Several nonsmoking ladies threatened to join in and increase the odds, but they were dissuaded, and by good staff work, or because the machine wanted oiling, the cigarette eventually stopped opposite the Minister.

Mr. Heath Robinson lit it with a Treasury match and presented it to his hostess. In gratitude she led the way to the kitchen, whence appetizing smells and healthy laughter were issuing.

Now, there are those who deplore the sacrifice of space and the expense of air-raid reinforcements. Some people deplore anything, except themselves—and others quickly remedy that deficiency.

Not so the Sensibles; they see obstacles as stepping stones and air-raid reinforcements as added opportunities.

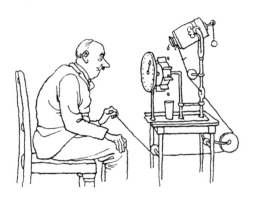

The "say when" machine for measuring war-time nips

Drawing lots for the cigarette

So Cook, who could not always keep up with the "16 to 60" Physical Jerks Squad in the Park, now does her daily dozen on the Chair Swing which has been hung from the struts. Martha, the maid, who is already fit and decidedly frolicsome, asked for a climbing rope to be hung from a beam. Its full use meant the removal of one electric light and the emptying of the glass cupboard on which she often landed, but these are small matters. Who would have thought of fitting anything for Martha in times of peace? You see the point?

You should see, too, the marvellous dinners which were served in this kitchen fortress. The reinforcements were no disfigurements, rather a delight. The beams were brought into the colour scheme, the struts were extended as seats. The whole effect was so stimulating that I found myself wondering what Sonia would do with a timberyard. But my thoughts were scattered by the real pleasures of sighting and seeking friends between the stanchions. Cliques and clusters were impossible and the occasional knocks and collisions only served to accentuate the delights of democracy.

After dinner the men joined Cyril Sensible in a pipe and a drink in the comfy coal-cellar. As will be seen from the Minister's quick sketch, it contains all that many men ask of life and much that the others don't get.

Making the best of things in the kitchen

When we rejoined the ladies we were dished out with our sand-bagged air-raid dressing-gowns. They were received with the hilarity accorded to carnival novelties.

Our hostess insisted that from experience it was wiser to don them for dancing so that interruptions could be taken in our stride.

The Minister, owing to abnormal cranial development, found difficulty in balancing the sand-bag headpiece, but Sonia swiftly extemporized with an Astrakan muff, which fitted lovingly. Unfortunately, it had not been in service since her great Aunt Amelia's time, and Sonia forgot to remove the moth balls. One lodged in the small of the Minister's back, but

Safe sociability

The comfy coal cellar

with a touch of genius and a maidenly blush, Sonia ordered a polka and almost at once the moth ball, an unidentifiable garment and the minutes of the last meeting made speedy appearance on the floor.

It was only when the relieved company called for a speech from the Minister to mark his safe recovery without operation, that we heard the siren. It was the "All Clear".

"Come again," Sonia said. "Other visitors will, so we shall make the best of things."

"Indeed we shall," the Minister said. "You are a national asset."

He bowed over her hand at parting. I have not seen him so moved since his budgerigar laid an egg on the Budget Box.

Sand-bagged dressing-gowns for shelters

Fire drill

TAILPIECE

The chief object in any war—after the enemy, of course—is to keep a sense of proportion. To imagine that you're the especial object of Hitler's hate or that every Fifth Columnist has your name and address embroidered on his body belt is just sheer and unwarrantable vanity. Far better refill the bitter-jug than be a jitter-bug.

Now in this little symphony of sense the Minister and I have sought to show what we've proved in practice, that in war there is a way of making the best of everything. You never know your luck!

It's so true. Think, for instance, of the dull days of the Boer War. What happened? The professional soldiers—which meant perhaps one man from every other street, two from the "Mermaid's Arms", and a company from Salisbury Plain—assembled by guile, gig or hay cart at some secret spot. There they were dished out with a special uniform designed to make them conspicuous among the canyons, kopjes, Krugers and other flora and fauna of a foreign land.

The more conscientious wives used the interval and the carbolic to clean out the bedroom, and the

Effective raid precaution by marked man

more hopeful sweethearts dusted the parlours in preparation for the return of the victors.

Meantime, the brave soldiers of the Queen were being heartily sick, while other men, less military but more controlled, were battling with bilges, doldrums, flying jibs and trade winds preparatory to landing our troops in South Africa.

When they arrived, which was about the time the wives started buying *With the Flag to Pretoria* in weekly parts, they deployed into the veldt. The veldt never seemed to be reasonably near at hand or even kind to the feet.

Mothers and wives of the potential heroes kept the martial spirit alive by draping Henry's or Archibald's photograph with a Union Jack and putting it in the centre of the mantelpiece between the fly-paper and the moustache cup.

Today, what progress! There are no privileged classes. Everyone is in it. What is more, everyone is at the Front. It simplifies matters considerably. But you should be equipped to meet all demands.

And mind you, that's not just a negative thing, like self-protection. It's positive—like spring onions or the answer to a maiden's prayer.

But the best preparation of all, the Minister has found, is to *think* positively from the moment of waking till the moment of sleeping. So we have devised a suggestive programme—or perhaps "tentative" would be less misunderstood. We find in our ministerial life that some people are so touchy about words outside their own vocabulary.

The programme begins at 7 a.m. because it must begin somewhere. But times can be altered as long as the programme is followed faithfully. It has been impossible, of course, to devise a typical day to suit both sexes, every age, climate, disposition and income, but the spirit is the thing and ample provision has been made for selection. The whole point is to follow the syllabus in spirit and in truth, because it is a scientifically balanced programme, chock full of the vital vitamins, and packed with hormones, peptones, cyclones and time lags. If you omit a single course, you destroy the balance. If you omit two courses you run grave risks of mental and physical disorder.

The Minister, for instance, has calculated that fourteen years and three months of every person's life are wasted by lying in bed after waking. Now, privately, I suspect the adding machine of inaccuracy because the Minister has a nervous habit of picking at it with a pin while he is telephoning; but supposing it is only *four* years and three months—something clearly must be done about it.

The Minister suggests that between 7 and 8 a.m. you should do a daily dozen (in the park or in your pyjamas), knit a body belt, dig a trench, fill in one

The poodle protector

Daily dozen

that somebody else is digging, send Greetings Telegrams to all those whose birthdays you have missed in the previous month, or part up with your secret stores of icing sugar. This can be most happily shaken over old razor blades, thereby making life more exciting for the salvage selectors.

Between 8 and 9 a.m. is the appointed time for fire drill, first-aid, flute obbligatos, repairing burst pipes, parachute patching, winding up clocks, putting the cat out, taking the milk in, doing *petit point* or studying Esperanto.

An interval is allowed about 8.10 a.m. for listening to the B.B.C. Programme Summary. This is essential in order to know what to avoid; otherwise much time can be lost by experiment.

From 9 till 12 is the chief work period. The morning is gold, the proverb says. This precious period should be devoted to manicure, tunny fishing, astronomy, hop scotch, paper tearing or cable laying.

From 12 till 1 p.m. has been scheduled by the Minister as the Contemplative Hour. Hitherto this hour has often been grossly misused, but total war is no time for the continuance of dubious habits. We are here to make the best of things, and that means following the Minister's plans wholeheartedly, if with an empty stomach.

The Contemplative Hour should be spent in one or more of the following pursuits: Pneumatic drilling, forestry, all-in wrestling, politics or blackmail. For

TAILPIECE

those under ten or over eighty, coal mining can be substituted for forestry in the first fifteen minutes.

The Minister, of course, does not merely employ the latest scientific research in the compilation of his programmes, he tests them upon normal human beings before they are put out.

He does not employ questionnaires, snoopers or coppers' narks. His method is far more subtle. Mr. Heath Robinson strolls across from Whitehall to St. James's Park and sits in the most comfortable free seat that overlooks the pelicans.

He then proceeds to scatter programmes idly upon the breeze. Some, if not all, are picked up, swept up, or sink in the lake.

Now inside each artfully decorated folder is a personal letter from the Minister telling the recipient that he or she has been personally selected from the five hundred million inhabitants of the British Empire to serve his or her country well and truly. Will he or she, Dear Sir or Madam, kindly follow the suggested programme for one day and then report fully to

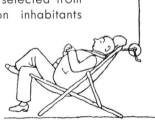

The contemplative hour in safety

123

Shrimping, if possible

the Ministry within seven days.

It is hinted, though not specifically stated (to avoid the taint of commercialism), that such services will be handsomely rewarded. There is also a clause indicating that pensions will be awarded to dependants if the programme should result in permanent disablement or fatal injuries.

From 1 till 2 is what the Minister has most happily named the Atmospheric Interlude. It is the self-expression period, so vital to our export trade and so productive of good in the individual. Each of the occupations suggested for this hour has been medically examined, tested for Aryan ancestry and stamped "P.T.O." on its most vulnerable feature.

These are the Atmospheric Activities from which to select your occupation for the witching hour of I till 2. MALES: Hat trimming, fossil cataloguing, figure skating, taking down carburettors, chimney sweeping, tea planting or carol singing. FEMALES: Butterfly breeding, pile driving, arctic exploration, glee singing, road repair or boll weevilling.

By 2 o'clock most healthy and able-bodied citizens are rested and ready for a further stretch of exercise.

The afternoon is best treated as a three-hour period, a peak period in the nation's harvest of

TAILPIECE

endeavour. It should be devoted to shrimping, collection of outstanding debts, limerick writing, foundation stone laying, splitting infinitives, or big game hunting.

Those with defective sight or weak insteps may find some of these listed occupations beyond their powers. For the purpose of this period, therefore, they can regard themselves as reserved occupations and should concentrate instead upon high diving, semaphoring, tattooing, punting or slate quarrying.

At 5 p.m., a period of approaching crisis, all equipment should be assembled, and hoes, stirrup pumps, sand, water, fenders and firearms and all scrap should be held at the "Ready".

From 5.15 to 5.30 p.m. the Minister calls the Transition Period, during which all equipment should be removed. After the half hour the normal peace-time business of the day begins— such things as eating, drinking, business, housework, and recreation. It is found that by concentrating such laudable but entirely incidental duties and pleasure into the few hours between 5.30 p.m. and bedtime the gastric juices are stimulated, and a healthy tiredness is encouraged.

Ready for any emergency

HEATH ROBINSON'S HOME FRONT

The Minister's files are congested with testimonials from those who in normal times are diffident about breakfast and only half-hearted about lunch. They record the relish with which they approach breakfast at 5.45 p.m. and the clearness of brain that results when approaching foreign travel, *petit point* or blackmail with an empty stomach.

As one over-zealous Duke said, after practising high diving in a slate quarry: "To think that it took a war to bring us to this!"

The Minister and I nodded, but of course we could accept no responsibility. We hold no brief for the war, as such. Indeed, it is sometimes a matter for internal grief with us that a conflict is necessary before our talents are given nation-wide scope.

We both, for instance, are more than natty at drawn-thread work; we both have a marked nobility of outline when seen in silhouette against the setting sun. Yet no one enlists these gifts or accords them publicity in times of peace. The only time anyone more important than a dog appeared interested was when the Minister absentmindedly took his stance upon a hill which in his youth had been a grassy mound, but which is now irrigated by trolley buses. But that was only a momentary diversion, for he was quickly moved, stance and all, to the local museum, where he passed unnoticed and was used as an umbrella rack.

Mind you, we do not complain; we merely state the truth. For, as Keats recorded, and as Heath Robinson and I are often reminded when we use our mirrors, "Beauty is truth, truth beauty—that is all ye know on earth, and all ye need to know."

TAILPIECE

Yet in our secret selves we do believe that in this book we have done something to make war more amenable and therefore we have brought peace appreciably nearer. We do not count on other rewards; at least, not openly. Not that we are unreceptive. The Minister would not reject a chest or two of tea, honestly come by and delivered at night, to supplement his strained ration. And I would not complain of fresh eggs, tactfully administered. Our other secret wants, in case any reader really falls for us are: *Heath Robinson*—Orpens, fountain pens, pipe cleaners, champagne in jeroboams, fresh fruit in due season; *Cecil Hunt*—Rembrandts, fountain pens, Stilton cheese, cider in casks, apples in all seasons. *Highgate, London*, will always find us, though with the removal of signboards we are not always sure of finding Highgate.

We do not expect to be included in the Honours List, though many a time in the creation of this work

The sand-bath for soap economy

we would have counted the mere apprehension of an enemy parachutist simple and joyous by comparison. But we do feel that by showing you and your kith and kin how to make the best of things, we have proved ourselves part of that inexplicable something which is for ever England.

If you will include us with the other contributory dumb animals when you toast "Victory" we shall be glad; and if you will leave a little at the bottom of the tankard we will arrange for it to be dredged and pipelined to Whitehall, and be gladder still.

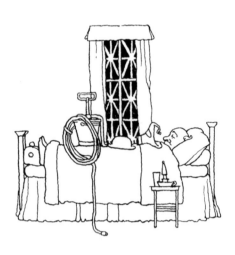

THE END